Y0-BEA-273

RA PRESS
100 Kennedy Drive #53
South Burlington, VT 05403
rapressrafilms.com

Acknowledgment and thanks to the following
journals where versions of some poems previously
appeared: *Adirondac:* "The Upper Great Range";
Adirondack Peeks: "Fourteen High Peak Facts";
Adirondack Trail: "High Peaks"; *Arc Poetry
Magazine*: "Slides"; *Blueline*: "Algonquin"; *Stone
Canoe*: "Water"; *The Adirondack Review*: "Gothics
via Orebed Brook"; *The Wayfarer*: "Big Slide" and
"The Santanonis"

Cover photograph: *From a Shoulder of Giant*
copyright © 2015 Nathan Farb

ISBN 978-1-312-84341-7

RA PRESS CHAPBOOK SERIES

High Peaks

David Crews

— March 2015 —

THE 46ERS

1. Mount Marcy | 5344
2. Algonquin Peak | 5114
3. Mount Haystack | 4960
4. Mount Skylight | 4926
5. Whiteface Mountain | 4867
6. Dix Mountain | 4857
7. Gray Peak | 4840
8. Iroquois Peak | 4840
9. Basin Mountain | 4827
10. Gothics | 4736
11. Mount Colden | 4714
12. Giant Mountain | 4627
13. Nippletop | 4620
14. Santanoni Peak | 4607
15. Mount Redfield | 4606
16. Wright Peak | 4580
17. Saddleback Mountain | 4515
18. Panther Peak | 4442
19. Table Top Mountain | 4427
20. Rocky Peak Ridge | 4420
21. Macomb Mountain | 4405
22. Armstrong Mountain | 4400
23. Hough Peak | 4400
24. Seward Mountain | 4361
25. Mount Marshall | 4360
26. Allen Mountain | 4340
27. Big Slide Mountain | 4240
28. Esther Mountain | 4240
29. Upper Wolfjaw Mountain | 4185
30. Lower Wolfjaw Mountain | 4175
31. Street Mountain | 4166

32. Phelps Mountain | 4161
33. Mount Donaldson | 4140
34. Seymour Mountain | 4120
35. Sawteeth | 4100
36. Cascade Mountain | 4098
37. South Dix (Carson Peak) | 4060
38. Porter Mountain | 4059
39. Mount Colvin | 4057
40. Mount Emmons | 4040
41. Dial Mountain | 4020
42. Grace Peak | 4012
43. Blake Peak | 3960
44. Cliff Mountain | 3960
45. Nye Mountain | 3895
46. Couchsachraga Peak | 3820

THE HIKES

Mileage and elevation gain of the subsequent hikes are estimates based on novice map reading, as well as the help of some websites, including cnyhiking.com and adirondack.net.

2 Jul 2012: Giant | 5.8 miles | 3050 feet elevation gain | 75, sunny, windy | Time in 11:10, out 15:30

4 Jul 2012: Big Slide | 9.5 miles | 2800 feet elevation gain | 85, sunny | Time in 9:40, out 19:00

6 Aug 2012: Gothics – Armstrong – Upper Wolfjaw | 14.6 miles | 4500 feet elevation gain | 75, mostly sunny | Time in 8:00, out 19:50

6 Oct 2012: Algonquin | 7.8 miles | 2950 feet elevation gain | 50, rain, sleet, & gusts | Time in 9:20, out 14:30

20-1 Oct 2012: Redfield | 19 miles | 3800 feet elevation gain | 55, partly sunny | Time in 8:30, out 11:30

27 Jun 2013: Giant – Rocky Peak Ridge | 10.5 miles | 4200 feet elevation gain | 80, partly sunny | Time in 8:30, out 17:10

28 Jun 2013: Porter – Cascade | 6.2 miles | 2200 feet elevation gain | 60, showers & gusts | Time in 10:30, out 14:40

15 Jul 2013: Macomb – South Dix (Carson) – Grace Peak – Hough | 13 miles | 4000 feet elevation gain | 90, sunny | Time in 6:50, out 15:30

23 Jul 2013: Table Top – Phelps | 13 miles | 3800 feet elevation gain | 75, showers | Time in 7:00, out 13:10

24 Jul 2013: Colvin – Blake | 14.6 miles | 4000 feet elevation gain | 65, partly cloudy | Time in 7:00, out 14:30

29 Jul 2013: Santanoni – Couchsachraga – Panther | 15.5 miles | 4950 feet elevation gain | 75, mostly sunny | Time in 6:30, out 14:50

31 Jul 2013: Allen | 17.8 miles | 2550 feet elevation gain | 75, mostly sunny | Time in 6:40, out 15:20

6 Aug 2013: Nippletop – Dial | 13.4 miles | 4000 feet elevation gain | 75, mostly sunny | Time in 7:00, out 13:30

12 Aug 2013: Colden | 13.4 miles | 2850 feet elevation gain | 75, partly cloudy | Time in 7:30, out 17:30

13 Aug 2013: Street – Nye | 8 miles | 2150 feet elevation gain | 65, showers | Time in 7:00, out 11:40

27 Aug 2013: Iroquois – Algonquin – Wright | 13.6 miles | 4150 feet elevation gain | 70, showers | Time in 7:30, out 15:00

29 Sep 2013: Esther – Whiteface | 10.2 miles | 3975 feet elevation gain | 65, sunny | Time in 7:30, out 12:40

8 Nov 2013: Marshall | 13.8 miles | 2575 feet elevation gain | 30, light snow | Time in 6:50, out 17:20

18 Jan 2014: Lower Wolfjaw | 10 miles | 2925 feet elevation gain | 30, mostly clear | Time in 7:00, out 17:20

16 May 2014: Dix | 13.6 miles | 3425 feet elevation gain | 60, rain & gusts | Time in 7:10, out 15:10

24 May 2014: Cliff – Gray – Skylight | 21.9 miles | 4950 feet elevation gain | 60, light showers | Time in 7:30, out 21:00

23 Jun 2014: Sawteeth – Gothics – Armstrong – Upper Wolfjaw | 16.9 miles | 5075 feet elevation gain | 80, mostly sunny | Time in 8:00, out 17:40

26 Jun 2014: Seymour | 13.6 miles | 2375 feet elevation gain | 80, partly sunny | Time in 8:30, out 15:20

28 Jun 2014: Haystack – Basin – Saddleback | 18.6 miles | 5825 feet elevation gain | 85, sunny | Time in 7:00, out 17:00

30 Jun 2014: Seward – Donaldson – Emmons | 17 miles | 3950 feet elevation gain | 80, mostly cloudy | Time in 7:50, out 16:20

2 Jul 2014: Marcy | 14.6 miles | 3525 feet elevation gain | 85, partly sunny | Time in 7:10, out 14:20

CONTENTS

On the afternoon of our arrival, and also the next morning, the view was completely shut off by the fog. But about the middle of the forenoon the wind changed, the fog lifted, and revealed to us the grandest mountain scenery we had beheld on our journey. There they sat about fifteen miles distant, a group of them,—Mount Marcy, Mount McIntyre, and Mount Golden, the real Adirondack monarchs.

John Burroughs, "The Adirondacks"

High Peaks

From Route 73 the bedrock rises
or maybe you rise. Cliff walls of conifer
loom into shale sky high
above the trailhead. These mountains
are new mountains made from old rocks
as the locals know though
traveling a million years back in time
the mind no longer accepts the story's
logic—dead-end, obscured view
and all that's left, trail—hard-pressed
dirt and rock snaking up and away
through maple and white cedar.
From the first false peak Giant's washbowl
glistens the way things glisten
at a distance and for a moment it seems
you could spit in it. Over the cliffs
space drops out, the open air now
with room to move about. On the summit
spin pirouettes like mountaintops
and see only blue sky sky sky.

Big Slide

You don't remember a hike you said
unless something burns you, grips
the soul. I remember humidity
and sweat, plodding our way through
an evergreen forest with trees so tall
we felt part of some other world
and the last three tenths of a mile up
Big Slide's slide with ladders and a hand
over hand climb that pulls you closer
and closer to those things you
thought you knew. Look, the Wolfjaws.
There's Gothics. It's a bit like an old friend
you say, and it's not crazy to talk
to the mountain, tell it what you're feeling
where you're hurting. And though I'm
almost sure my buddy's head contains its own
unique bedrock, something tells me
his instincts prove ancient and the forest
echoes voices, some lifting above
falling mountain streams.

Gothics via Orebed Brook

The idea of the slide, the ladders,
the cable, the cliffwalking, probably
stings more than the bee itself. Still
there was no shame turtling up the peak
of Gothics, far below a graveyard of trees
remnants from last year's hurricane.
At 4736 feet above sea level
anything seems possible. Your boots grow
wings and the urge to touch the sun
is there. Spires now visible from the summit
of Armstrong, at Upper Wolfjaw
it was all Giant. There's something about
these mountains, the glacier carved deep
valleys, ridges rising together, peaks
so close they bring an intimacy
to the landscape. And just as quickly
you drop down into dark forest and see
these woods dwell in another element
and if you stop walking, listen
the silence reverberates back.

Algonquin

First called Mount McIntyre after
an Archibald who owned and operated
McIntyre Iron Works and served
as Controller of New York State
Algonquin Peak later received
its name from a one Verplanck Colvin
who conducted a survey of the mountain
region around 1873. I like to imagine
the Algonquin people calling it
"One Who Hides In Clouds" or "She
Who Collects Rain," for
our ascent showed no lookouts
to Whiteface or Lake Placid. We did not
see the trees turning rusty orange
did not feel the crisp autumn air
licking our hair. We hiked in clouds
and rain for over seven miles up nearly
three thousand feet for Jane's birthday
and at the summit the wind gusts
nearly blew us off the mountain.

Redfield

Many hikes in the High Peaks
require four, five, even six or seven
miles of trailwalking just to land
at the base of a climb. Forget the
cell phone. These mountains don't exist
in real time. For thousands of years
these trails have been tucking
themselves between ridges, hiding
in valleys, deep within the six million
acres of Adirondack wilderness. This place
is why people make waterproof matches.
Don't hike without a roll of tape, a water
filter. To underestimate could mean
stranded for a night, an uncomfortable
stay in the woods. And don't always expect
romantic mountain vistas for it rains here
all the time, could snow any part
of the year. The herdpath up Redfield begins
behind the Uphill Lean To and it's about
a mile and a half to the summit.

Trail Confessions

It's not until you see the next false
peak that you realize there's a next
false peak, kind of like the space
between falling out and in love again.
There's actually three on Giant
and the bedrock offers such incredible
grip it's no wonder it tore apart
Murphy's pads. On these summits
over four thousand feet I feel the need
to steady the legs, it can get a little
shaky if you let it. It's a plunge to the saddle
before Rocky Peak Ridge and I'll
take it slow since no one's watching.
Slip a step and you'd take a dive, break
a leg for sure. I think of these things.
Think about lightning strikes, about
losing it on a ridgewalk—would I hit
the head, land in some trees. At home
a carrot or two helps sweeten the sauce.
I usually sit down when I pee.

Cascade and Porter

Somewhere between all that is
and all that won't ever be, the rain.
Even in nature things can only take
so much. At some point
saturation. Water pours out crevices
in rock, water runs down the trail, water
drips from leaves. Down in Keene
Valley they're about ready to close
Route 73 at Hulls Falls Road, the East
Branch of the Ausable River looks like
a theme park ride. Some houses sit
with water to the steps and more
showers are expected. Near the trailhead
to Cascade then Porter mountain water
falls, collects into a strong, tumbling brook
we must either ford or return to the car.
The trail's sequestered with crashed trees
washed down from the last storm, some
so big they'd take seven or eight people
to lift. Never even considered a flash flood.

The Dix Range

Herdpaths are here Tom says
because people like us have hiked them,
each step shapes the way. The Forty-Sixers
also help maintain many of what the state
calls—"wilderness paths"—trailless peaks
require. If you go it alone you need not worry
about blazes, look for cairns. If you read
ahead a col is a ridge between two peaks,
a saddle a drop. If you don't know orienteering
you're probably without a compass anyway.
The summit's the grail. You'll know at once
up the slide of Macomb, you'll know up Hough.
It's only Grace Peak if we refuse to name
mountains after politicians and businessmen.
It's only Carson Peak if we stand at the summit
and talk about the writers of this region,
the women who first hiked these trails.
The white-throated sparrow claiming
his space on this ridge also reminds us
there are others who call these hills home.

Fourteen High Peak Facts

There's no such thing as showers
in the High Peaks, only rain. No mountain
of four thousand feet is a small mountain.
Talking to yourself, a sign of intelligence.
Waterproof is not a real word, everything's
soaked by mile four. Your boots
the most important piece of gear. The best
twelve bucks you'll ever spend, a headnet.
Rocks are almost never slippery (even
when wet). Maps don't lie, the way up's longer.
A songbird will alert you to the summit, perhaps
a blackburnian warbler, a wood thrush, or if
you're lucky, a field sparrow. By mile ten you
and your clothes will smell like swamp. Every
trail has its own personality. The herdpath up
Table Top must be a river most the year. I bet
the view from Phelps gives a good payoff.
On many hikes in the High Peaks expect
the clouds to break and the sun to shine
roughly eight tenths of a mile from your car.

Verplanck Colvin

In 1872, Verplanck Colvin, newly
appointed Secretary of New York State
Park Commissions and his lifelong friend
Mills Blake, named assistant in charge
Divisions of Levels, embarked on a project
to survey the mountain region of higher
New York. In snow and ice, sun, rain, setting up
deep camps through frozen temperatures, Colvin
and his men climbed hundreds of mountains
using theodolites to cover the region in a vast
network of triangles, noting contours in the land
where rivers fell, lakes hid, using shiny tin
devices to level measurements of summits
above the sea. It was in and around these years
when Colvin's work put in motion a series
of actions that would preserve the wild that is
the High Peaks, not to mention collecting
thousands upon thousands of calculations
in order to create a map of the region
without which any hiker would be lost.

The Santanonis

"What was the region northward still?"
the white men asked the Indians. It was
the *Cough-sa-gra-ga.* Four hundred years ago
when Hudson and Champlain traveled up
these rivers into the heart of this untamed
wilderness, the Mohican and the Iroquois
and the Algonquin had no way of reaching
India. And after the indian savage were
driven backward, deeper, into the dark hinter
land the High Peaks were decimated by logging
and the rise of the big business tycoons that would
later become this country. Only seven miles
from the car though far behind a ridgeline
that holds Panther and Santanoni and walls high
above, the herdpath feels wild and untamed
and for a moment that time of no time comes
back to me. A time before logging trucks and
highways, before gas stations and billboards.
Wachshu in Mohican means mountain.
Imagine all the mountains had one name.

Allen, aka The Loneliest Mtn.

One often finds Adirondack trails
not heavily traveled though passing
fellow hikers usually proves a pleasant
experience as a certain congeniality
seems to exist between individuals who
share the commons. Hiking's relatively
free. The journey taxes the body
and the mind. And we share the mud, share
the rocks and blackflies, the heat
and sun. It's a trudge for miles through
nowhere and a serious climb once
at the base near Allen Brook.
The red slime's for real—couldn't
imagine climbing in rain—you'd slip
right off the damn mountain. On the top
no real lookouts. Someone tried to
steal the sign at the summit and broke it.
Hidden among trees with its broken
sign stands Allen Mountain, also
known as *The Loneliest Mtn.*

Nippletop's Top

When the weather's right on an open
summit the map helps paint the view.
Some ridgelines so dramatic they need
names like The Great Range. And
from the top of Nippletop one need not
be Verplanck Colvin to figure a difference
between a peak, a mount, and a mountain.
Mount Marcy, Mount Haystack, Mount
Skylight command a presence. Santanoni
Peak, Couchsachraga Peak, Hough Peak
are hauls to the top. And Dix Mountain,
Allen Mountain, Redfield Mountain claim
a prominence. Though too much pattern exists
not to suggest poetry as well plays a role
in the naming. Panther Peak? Blake Peak?
Basin Mountain? We need the music like we
need freedom to hike or breathe. Dial's lookout
makes these hills old friends, some of whom
need no introduction—Gothics, Saw
teeth, or Jane's favorite, Nippletop.

Trail Etiquette

Peeing directly on the trail
generally frowned upon. And you
might not want to hear this
but you have to bury shit. Litter
defines itself as anything left
by another human being that would
not normally be found in the ecosystem.
Yes, orange peels are organic material
and should be carried out. People hiking
up hold the right of way. It's important
to walk through the mud, especially
in an alpine zone. Asking how far
to Colden's summit defeats the spirit
of being in the woods. (Hike quietly.)
If taking a break, move off the trail.
While carving yours and your
sweetheart's initials into a giant
elm tree will ensure the two of you
will remain in love forever, consider
instead leaving no trace.

Moss

The herdpath leaves Heart Lake
winding its way toward the brook
of Indian Pass, across where it turns
into denser woods, climbs slowly at first
then rises inside a mountain stream
toward the ridge and the juncture between
Nye and Street. After a few tenths of a mile
and nearing four thousand feet, Street
morphs into Moss Mountain, into
the Museum of Moss, no, into the
Adirondack High Peaks Botanical Garden
of Moss. There exists over twelve
thousand species of moss, all of which
might reside on Street Mountain. There
moss grows on rocks, on boulders, moss
snakes up trees, moss covers all
of the ground, in the ferns, except where
the herdpath muds its way through a forest
of green. Hope for light rain, clouds
at the summit. Bring a jacket.

Slides

Ducking and weaving and climbing
the way toward Avalanche Pass, broken
and splintered trees pile high, crisscross
at the trail's edge, and give glimpses of this
continually changing mountain landscape.
High above, even in early light, the clear
white rock on one of Colden's new slides
shines. With enough rain, in the middle
of a dark night, soil saturated beyond hold
eventually gives way, mud and rock and
trees all fall deafening the mountainside.
Most trails up these peaks follow exposed
bedrock where water carves paths
through the timberline. Up Iroquois, clouds.
Up Algonquin again, clouds. But after
the scramble toward Wright's rocky peak
the thick and rolling moisture blew apart
to reveal the jagged scars of Colden's steep
face and in the distance Marcy's broad
shadow rising inside a gutted sky.

Whiteface

Back again. Perhaps the last go
of summer. I wake to the bark
and howl of coyotes above Paradox
Lake, their wild dalliances in the blue
black chill of morning. It's the start
of one of those days, the stillness
that sets in before the dying season.
Chapel Pond sits nestled against cliffs,
a sheet of glass. Up Marble Mountain
light breaks through yellowed birch trees,
a quartered moon clings to blue sky.
In the distance thick fog settles in the valleys
of the High Peaks. I weave and dodge
and cut through the trail and on Esther's
summit Whiteface looms showered
in sepia, amber, crimson, pine. My legs go
slack at the image of climbing the ridgeline,
the view will be miles. At the top
I take off my boots, socks, and listen
as people call out the mountains they see.

The Marshall Brothers

Two brothers, Robert and George
Marshall, and their guide, family friend
Herbert Clark, between the years 1918 and
1925 set off to hike the forty-six highest
mountains in New York's Adirondack
State Park. Although recent surveys down
graded certain summit levels, while raising
others—like McNaughton—above the mark
the forty-six peaks they climbed remain
the peaks of The 46ers, stipulations of which
include a mountain summit above four thousand
feet, at least three hundred feet elevation
at the apex, separated from the next closest
peak by more than three quarters of a mile.
(The moleskin used to tape reddening blisters
need not be actual mole skin.) In these
years, these individuals found few maintained
trails to summits. No trailmarkers, no ladders,
no signs. Just deep wilderness on all sides
and the pine trees with their hush and sighs.

Lower Wolfjaw

Just above the path at Rooster Comb
trailhead to Lower Wolfjaw a full moon
plasters an orange glow all over Big Slide,
the Brothers, too, frozen in morning snow.
These senses in winter so clear, magnified.
And oh how nature's order and disorder
always seems logical and right. Still
it's difficult to ever know what the mountain
will give you. A warm stretch, thaw, snowmelt
and a deep freeze—it's here, where you could
find yourself climbing cliffs of solid ice,
your microspikes not nearly enough utility
to keep from sliding off the mountain. There
Tom says, see that ledge? It's a thousand feet
down on the other side. Slip and fall, and you're
having a bad day. These are the moments
I assure my mother do not exist. When the
tension of adventure beckons while your gut
wrapped warmly inside layers of wool
finds itself clutching trees for serious life.

Water

What the woods are. What the green
looks like. When it sounds. How the packed
soil hardens under each boot. How the rocks
smoothed. How the rain hits the face.
Whether the spruce clings to the creek's
edge. If the beaver dam holds. Why the mud.
Before and after the memory of ice
freezing, splitting rock. When the moss grip,
listen. How the hemlock rise, darken. How the trail
dips, turns, sinks, climbs. Why the river
falls. How the slide is carved. When the melt
rushes the mountain. While the summit winds
whip the balsam fir. Huddled in my knees
between gaps in the bedrock atop Dix Mountain
I stare into the pure moisture of gusting
clouds, behold this gigantic rock rainforest.
And later, descending back upon blazed
trail, when the black-throated green warbler
shrills tzee tzee zoozee hidden
in the birch canopy. Why the solitary loon.

Dream Hikes

The trailhead's empty. Not a car in sight.
Tom's here, but he's not. I hear his voice
and he says he hears my thoughts. Inside
the logbook I scratch down our names,
the town where we live, Jane's phone number.
I do not write the mountains we plan to hike
but draw their ridges rising, blot a finger
of dirt to brush the evergreens, smooth the mud
before Cliff's second summit, edge Marcy's
bedrock through the trees on Gray, soften
the bowl of light above Skylight. Climbing
the trail to Four Corners water rages down
Feldspar Brook, the same water that one day
will filter into New York Bay. Colvin called it
a tear of the clouds. On hands and knees I stare
into water, touch two skies, walk two ridgelines,
view two mountain summits. On Skylight's
broad top a wall of dark gray moisture swallows
Marcy's peak and when the hail begins falling
it falls in almost straight lines from the sky.

Sawteeth

Trekking the Lake Road from Saint
Huberts not a new thing, access to the
High Peaks returns me again and again
to familiar trailheads—Upper Works,
Adirondack Loj, Johns Brook. The Scenic
Trail to Sawteeth twists and turns up
the mountainside, popping out to a rocky
overlook, ducking back into the woods.
Catch it right means I get to embrace
some private moments—a turkey
vulture thermal lifting over a ledge that
drops off into a sunlit Lower Ausable Lake,
the Colvin Range running toward
the wild and distant Marcy Swamp, Pyramid
Peak heightening Gothics. The allure
of perspective brings me back. And once
high, mountain peaks cut the horizon in
every direction, the view that carries you
to Armstrong then Upper Wolfjaw. Why
don't you take pictures, people ask.

Deprivation

There's something about it—not having
shelter from rain, from nature's elements.
Nothing to turn off humidity, nothing to
stop me from getting webbed. If lulled
into the moment I might step on a wet
tree trunk, slip and fall, maybe scrape up
my forearm. On my birthday, no less. It's
the stench of sweat and mud, wet socks. Hiking
up the wrong herdpath, a mile out of the way.
My legs always climbing and climbing. The pain
on the outside of my right knee, the sore and tired
balls of the feet. And the mosquitoes, the goddamn
mosquitoes. When the sun comes out on Seymour
it bears down with a thousand oppressive
thoughts. But as soon I'm back at the car, back
home again. A shower turns to purgation. To sit
in a chair like a coronation. The first sip of beer
hits with the bitter tang of hops. And the steak
so tender I could've kissed that steer on the head
right before the bolt pistol.

The Upper Great Range

These are some of the big ones, deep
in the Upper Great Range. The night before
I had difficulty sleeping, scaling over and
over the cliffs of my mind. I'm no extreme
junky. I read poetry, enjoy birds. And yet
climbing the trail from Bushnell Falls toward
Haystack my boots feel light, my feet right
in them. I traverse mud, leaping from rock
to rock, leaning on my poles, remembering
a time when I was ten and spent most
the summer jumping the creek behind
Wolf Hill Elementary, coming home muddy
each and every afternoon. (That still
happens.) Do not pass this point, the sign
reads, unless if a child again. By the time
I begin the ascent of Basin my mind races
with adrenaline as I try to recall at what
angle the boot no longer grips wet bedrock.
I think too much. A child would not fear
the cliffs of Saddleback, so the poem goes.

The Sewards

According to Colvin around the year
1840 the region came to be known as
the Adirondack Mountains after the last
Indian dwelling inside its rocky ridges.
The name given by a Professor Ebenezer
Emmons who around that time completed
the first geological survey of the state. In
1870, at the age of twenty-three, Colvin made
an ascent of Seward Mountain striking as he says
a northeasterly course, hitting first a smaller
summit, later named Donaldson, in an attempt
to register its barometric pressure. His findings
were published the next year in an essay in which
Colvin warned the state that intensified logging
would increase the rate of snowmelt, ultimately
draining the supply of water to the cities of Albany
and New York. Two years later he was given ten
hundred dollars to survey the region. Nothing
it seems is without an opportunity cost. Even
now the mountains sit there, waiting.

High Peaks

Otherwise known as *Tahaws* or "Cloud-
Splitter," Mount Marcy stands 5344 feet
above sea level, nestled in the heart of the
High Peaks. It was named in 1837 when the first
recorded ascent was commissioned by
the governor. Standing now at the summit, turning
and turning at the top of the world, a hundred
names flood my mind—Panther Gorge, Elk
Lake, Caribou Pass, Klondike Notch, Pinnacle—
there's a music to this place, and I want to listen
more. I want to hear the songbirds hiding in the
balsam fir, the broadwings cry. I want to hear
the wind whip the summit grasses, hear streams
rush down the mountainside, hear the rain
fall. (Here, I want to stay.) The Adirondacks
rise one mile high, a hundred and sixty across.
There are over two thousand miles of trail
snaking through the park. You know how it is—
to find me again look under your bootsoles.
There's a music even in the mud. Listen for it.

NOTES

The book's epigraph comes from an essay written in 1866 by John Burroughs titled "The Adirondacks," first published in the collection *Wake-Robin* (1871), and is found in *Deep Woods* edited by Richard F. Fleck (Syracuse University Press, 1998).

"The Dix Range" includes references made to both Grace Hudowalski (1906-2004), the ninth person and first woman to climb all forty-six of the Adirondack High Peaks, and Russell M.L. Carson (1884-1961), author of *People and Peaks of the Adirondacks*; on June 12 of 2014 the grass roots movement to rename East Dix to Grace Peak reached success when the U.S. Board of Geographic Names voted to approve the change, while South Dix has yet to be officially renamed Carson Peak. For more information on The Adirondack Forty-Sixers (and where the sea level heights were found for the front matter) please visit adk46er.org. For more on the life and times of Grace Hudowalski, who spent decades as Historian of the Forty-Sixer organization, nurturing its community of hikers through a continued personalized correspondence, please see the documentary *The Mountains Will Wait For You: A Tribute to Grace Hudowalski* (Summit Pictures LLC, 2013). Special thanks to the Historic Museum at Colonial Gardens in Elizabethtown, New York for their special exhibit on Ms. Hudowalski, personally viewed in July of 2014.

"Verplanck Colvin" history and information on work and life from "The Adirondack Survey," as well as other writings included in *Adirondack Explorations: Nature Writings of Verplanck Colvin* edited by Paul Schaefer (Syracuse University Press, 2000).

"The Santanonis" includes lines (the first three) from Verplanck Colvin's "The Adirondack Survey" (*Adirondack Explorations: Nature Writings of Verplanck Colvin*, Syracuse University Press, 2000). A Mohican Dictionary compiled by Lion G. Miles can be found at mohican-nsn.gov.

"Allen, aka The Loneliest Mtn." refers to the verbiage found written on a piece of tape on Allen Mountain's broken summit signage. Speaking to a gentleman—also a Forty-Sixer—on the summit of Couchsachraga, he mentioned how individuals stealing summit signs have been a problem of late. He felt if trail mileage and directional information were added to these signs, perhaps some people would be less inclined to take them.

"Trail Etiquette" references Mount Colden and perhaps necessitates a return to the epigraph and Burroughs's essay, "The Adriondacks." The U.S. Geological Survey still denotes the range of Mount Marshall, Iroquois Peak, Algonquin Peak, and Wright Peak with the spelling "MacIntyre;" the plaque on Mount Marcy also includes that same spelling. In 1871 Burroughs would be accurate to call Algonquin Peak— "McIntyre"—and followed the correct spelling of the Iron Works owner and operator. He did, however, probably miswrite "Golden" (a name of which I could find no history). His view from Lower Iron Works, on a trail toward Long Lake, would give him a northeasterly view where one would most likely see Marcy, McIntyre (Algonquin), and Mount Colden, not "Golden."

"The Marshall Brothers" references the lives of Bob, George Marshall and Herbert Clark, as well as their early Adirondack High Peak mountaineering, information of which can be found in George Marshall's "Preface," as well as under Carson's section for "Mount Marshall" in

40

the Adirondack Mountain Club's 1986 reprint of Russell M.L. Carson's *People and Peaks of the Adirondacks* (Doubleday, Doran & Company, Inc., 1927). Other interesting information on the life and times of the Marshall brothers and Herbert Clark can be found in the writings of Bob Marshall, especially "The High Peaks of the Adirondacks" in *Bob Marshall in the Adirondacks: Writings of a Pioneering, Peak-Bagger, Pond-Hopper, and Wilderness Preservationist* edited by Phil Brown (Lost Pond Press, 2006).

"Dream Hikes" references Lake Tear of the Clouds, discovered, written about, and named by Verplanck Colvin: "As a matter of technical interest, the discovery of the true highest pond-source of the Hudson river is, perhaps, more interesting. Far above the chilly waters of Lake Avalanche, at an elevation of 4,293 feet, is *Summit Water*, a minute, unpretending tear of the clouds—as it were—a lonely pool, shivering in the breezes of the mountains, and sending its limpid surplus through Feldspar brook to the Opalescent river, the wellspring of the Hudson" (*Adirondack Explorations: Nature Writings of Verplanck Colvin*, Syracuse University Press, 2000).

"The Sewards" references Verplanck Colvin's essays "The Adirondack Survey" and "Ascent of Mount Seward and Its Barometrical Measurement," the second of which was published by the New York Board of Regents in 1871 (*Adirondack Explorations: Nature Writings of Verplanck Colvin*, Syracuse University Press, 2000). Also from Russell M.L. Carson: "The first ascent of Mount Donaldson was incidental to the earliest ascent of Mount Seward, which was the goal of the climbers. A careful study of Colvin's account of the pioneer exploration of the Seward Mountains by himself and his guide, Alvah Dunning, indicates that they were on top of Mount

Donaldson late in the afternoon of October 14, 1870, the day before they reached the summit of Mount Seward" (*People and Peaks of the Adirondacks,* Doubleday, Doran & Company, Inc., 1927). Carson's book also makes reference to *A History of the Adirondacks* by Alfred L. Donaldson (BiblioBazaar, reproduced in 2009).

"High Peaks" penultimate line plays off of the final lines of Walt Whitman's "Song of Myself" (*Leaves of Grass,* 1855). Also there is a plaque on Mount Marcy which gives information on the mountain's other names, as well as the members of the hiking party who made the first recorded ascent. In addition, see Alfred L. Donaldson's poem "The Song of Tahawus" included in *People and Peaks of the Adirondacks* by Russell M.L. Carson (Doubleday, Doran & Company, Inc., 1927).

Other interesting historical and geological information on the Adirondack High Peaks can be found in the following personal accounts: *The Adirondacks* by T. Morris Longstreth (Black Dome, reprinted in 2005 from 1917 original) and *Woodswoman* by Anne LaBastille (Penguin, 1991 from the E.P Dutton, 1978 original).

Other information on New York's Adirondack State Park from apa.ny.gov.

As of 2015 the Forty-Sixers organization includes 8,816 registered individuals who have climbed these forty-six peaks.

ACKNOWLEDGMENTS

Thank you to those individuals who offered readings of these poems, including: Carey Albertine, Ralph Caiazzo, Josh Gebhart, Joe Geddes, Darla Himeles, Rebecca Gayle Howell, Tom Koehler, Jane Larsen, Paul Milan, Roger Mitchell, Tom Napier, Priscilla Orr, Anthony Pittala, Lisa Varisco, and Judith Vollmer. Roger and Judith, especially, for sharing your thoughts and reflections about the manuscript for the back cover.

To my father and mother (and to whom this book is dedicated), who listened to countless live readings and stories of adventure, thank you for the love, support, guidance. You mean more to me than you know.

Also, thank you to my friends and family for showing your care (especially, my mother) when you would share with me your concerns I might fall off a mountain.

Thank you to Nathan Farb who has not only showed me great generosity, but has provided such a beautiful cover photo. You are an inspiration to those who cherish The Adirondacks.

Please, a warm thank you to those individuals who venture into the woods (especially, the Forty-Sixers) to provide trail maintenance and upkeep, so others can enjoy its solace and beauty.

Also, a recognition to those with whom these trails have been shared, especially: our hippie friends (on the summit of Big Slide); Monty from Maryland (at the top of Table Top); the father-son running duo from Buffalo (on the trail toward Avalanche Pass); our 46er friends (on Couchi); Luke (on Algonquin then Wright); my fellow New Jersey teacher buddies Jake, Alex, and Becca (on the saddle between Sawteeth and Pyramid, then over

Gothics); Brian, Max, and Kevin enjoying Max's first 46er (on Seymour); Erin and John (on Haystack then Basin); Warren (on Donaldson and Emmons); Drew, the Summit Steward (on Marcy); and especially Nanette and Anthony (who accompanied a hiking party up Big Slide and Dix, respectively).

Finally, a sincere gratitude please to my two hiking partners: Tommy, who provided so much of the enthusiasm and inspiration to climb these hills, and to Jane (who loves Murphy) and knows not how to meet a challenge and say no.

ABOUT THE AUTHOR

DAVID CREWS (davidcrews*poetry*.com) has a collection of poems titled *Circadian Rhythm* published with The Paulinskill Poetry Project (2014). His poems have appeared in *The Southeast Review, Berkeley Poetry Review, The Carolina Quarterly*, *Wisconsin Review, Paterson Literary Review,* and others. Essays found in *Adanna Literary Journal* and *SPECTRUM.* He has twice been nominated for a Pushcart Prize. Crews received an MFA in Poetry from Drew University, serves as managing editor for *The Stillwater Review,* and both teaches and lives in northwest New Jersey.

Photograph by Barbara Tripi